Goal:
The intent children and young adults to embrace life and death as a natural part of God's creation.

Inspiration:
Inspiration came from the many children and young adults who demonstrated great courage while their loved ones faced a life-threatening illness. Their fantastic ability to ask questions, openly share concerns and feelings, and willingness to explore new areas of life and death, contributed greatly to their healing and the inspiration of this book. Without them this book would not have been possible.

About the author:
Stephanie A. Jonah is a registered nurse, currently working in hospice. She has worked for many years with children and adults, in a variety of settings including hospitals, hospice, as a guest speaker for children whose parents have a life-threatening illness, home visits, and volunteering in a Romanian orphanage.

Acknowledgments:
It is with great gratitude, that I extend my thanks to everyone who touched my heart and made this book possible. A special thanks to supportive friends, family, and colleagues for assisting me with the editing and production of this book.

God Bless You.

Presented by:

_____

This activity book

belongs to:

_____

Hello Friend,

    This is your own special activity book. Someone you know is very sick and may die. You might have a few questions about death, and I want to help you. Together, we can explore our feelings and share our questions about life and death.

    You can draw, color, and write in your special activity book.

    You may share it if you want to, or keep it for your eyes only. The choice is yours.

God Bless You.

In the Spirit of Love,

I AM

Your Friend.

# Transitions Along the Way

A Guide to the Dying Process
for Children and Young Adults

Stephanie A. Jonah, R.N.

Visions
Fairfield, California

Published by
Visions
3165 Orchard View Drive
Fairfield, California 94533

Copyright 1999 by Stephanie A. Jonah, R.N.

All rights reserved unconditionally throughout the world, including foreign translation. No part of this work may be reproduced or copied in any form or by any means — graphic, electronic, or mechanical, including photocopying, recording, taping, or by information storage and retrieval systems — without written permission of the publisher.

ISBN: 0-9671487-7-4

Printed in the United States of America

10 9 8 7 6 5 4 3 2 1

Is there someone in your life who is sick and may die? I remember the first time I saw someone who was sick and dying, I was very scared.

I did not know what to expect. I did not know what was going to happen. That is why I was so scared. It's OK to be scared.

I had so many different feelings which at times hurt a lot. Sometimes I was angry. Sometimes I felt sad and cried. Sometimes I felt happy. And sometimes I felt so confused I couldn't tell you what I was feeling. How do you feel right now?

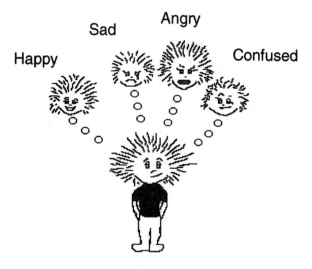

I wondered if it was normal to have so many feelings. I was told I would have many, many different feelings, and this was to be expected. **Feelings are not right or wrong, they are just feelings.**

Draw or write about something that makes you feel angry, since the person you love got sick. It's OK to feel angry.

I wondered what changes I would see when someone is getting close to dying. I wanted to know what happens when the body dies? How long would it take? Do you ever think about these questions? I had so many questions.

So I talked to my mom and dad, the doctors, and the nurses. I shared all my questions with them, even the ones that seemed silly. After all, we all know: there are no silly questions.

I remembered some pretty mean things I had said when I was real angry. I wondered if the mean things I had said made the person sick and was now causing their death.

Everyone told me that even though I had said some mean things in the past, **I was not the cause of their sickness or their death.** This was very important for me to remember.

Draw or write about something you wish you had not said to the person you love. It's OK.

I learned so much from all the questions I asked. I wrote down the answers so I could share them with you!

Maybe it will help you if I answer some of the questions you have about death and dying. Can you think of any questions?

## What changes do you see when someone is getting close to death?

Draw or write about the changes you think you might see when someone is getting close to death. Can you think of any changes?

When people are close to death, many things may change in their lives. I will talk about those changes in just a minute. Before I do, I want to share something with you that I learned which is very, very important:

whether people are healthy, very sick, or dying, **we all want one thing, and that is to be loved.**

**Your love is the greatest gift you can give and share.** When you are sick, people take care of you because they love you. They may even say they love you and hope you feel better soon. This usually makes you feel all warm and fuzzy inside.

**It's a good feeling.**

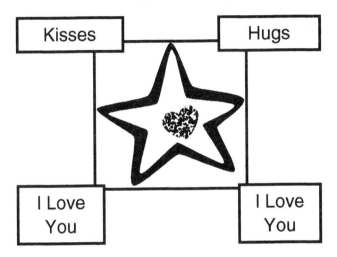

People who are dying also want to be loved. They also get that warm and fuzzy feeling inside when you say you love them, give them hugs and kisses, or spend time with them. You will not catch their sickness and die by doing this. You can give them all the hugs and kisses you want and say **"I love you"** 100 times. It is **safe** to do this and you will make them very happy.

# LOVE

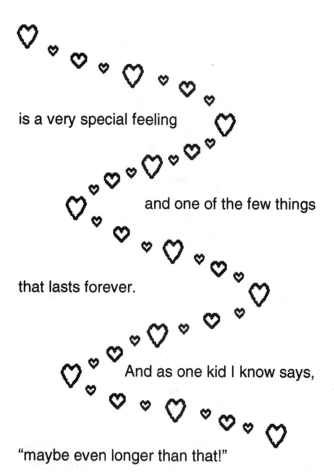

is a very special feeling

and one of the few things

that lasts forever.

And as one kid I know says,

"maybe even longer than that!"

Draw or write about love.

Now let's see,

back to the first question.

What changes do you see when people are getting close to death? There are so many changes that may happen. I will tell you about the most common changes you might see.

Dying people may not eat as much food as they used to. Sometimes they don't feel hungry, or they might feel too sick to eat. They might even refuse to eat their favorite food.

| Is the sick person you know losing weight? |

"My pants are too big. I'm lucky I have suspenders to hold up my pants!"

Some people lose a lot of weight and have trouble with the way their clothes fit.

They may feel like their muscles are getting weaker and they are losing their strength.

Things they did before easily, like walking, lifting things, playing, cooking, taking a shower or bath, may become hard for some people to do because they feel so weak. They may even feel too weak to do their favorite things. Have you noticed any changes?

Draw or write about something you miss doing with the person you love.

In time, they may become so weak and tired that they can't get out of bed. It just takes too much energy. They are so tired that **they do everything in bed.**

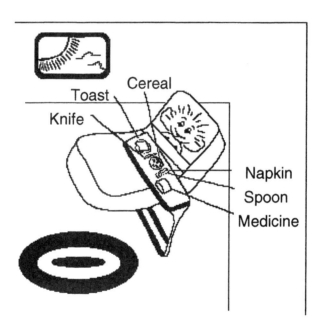

They may eat breakfast, lunch, dinner, snacks, and dessert in bed. Let's hope they don't spill anything! That would be quite a mess to clean up!

**It happens sometimes, you know.**

## Bath time

They may have someone give them a sponge bath in bed. We don't really use a sponge, though.

A sponge bath is usually done using warm water, a washcloth, soap, and a dry towel. It works really well once you get the hang of it. **It feels really good, too!**

When sick people are awake, they may read a book, write letters, play, draw, paint, listen to music, talk in bed, and do many other things. This might be a good chance for you to spend time together.

Sometimes people are too sick to talk. You can still share your feelings with them. Their hearing still works.

**Draw or write about something you would like to say or do with the person who is sick.**

They may also go to the bathroom in bed.

Well, not exactly in bed.

They usually go in a

Bedpan ➡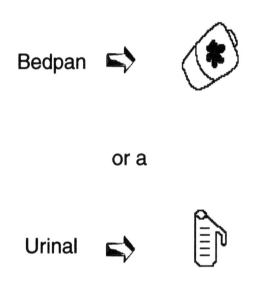

or a

Urinal ➡

Men and women and boys and girls may all use a bedpan. The urinal may be used by men and boys only. Have you ever seen a bedpan or a urinal?

Sometimes people don't know they have to go to the toilet, or might feel too weak to get there in time.

They might even wet the bed!

It's OK. It happens, you know!

When this happens, they might have to wear a diaper. Did you know there are diapers for babies, children, and adults? Adult diapers are just like baby diapers, except they are **much bigger!** Do you know anyone who wears diapers?

Diapers come in all sizes.

Baby — Adult — Child

**As time passes,**

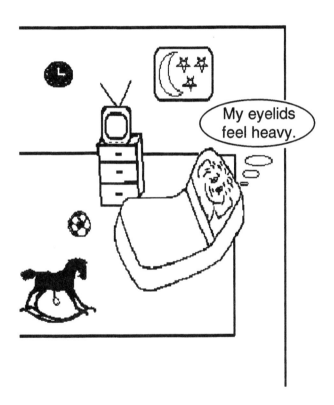

They might feel **very tired** and find it hard to keep their eyes open.

They may sleep more and more.

**Sleep, sleep, sleep.**

You probably thought only babies or bears in hibernation slept that much. Does the sick person you know sleep a lot?

Draw or write about how you feel about someone you love being so sick. It's OK.

|  |
|---|
| Peaceful |
| Angry                    Scared |
| Sad                      Guilty |
| Happy                    Lonely |
| Confused |

# What happens when the body dies?

Write or draw about what you think happens when the body dies. Do you have any ideas?

Death is often shown in cartoons as a scary looking person who comes to get people who are dying. This is only a cartoon, and we all know that cartoons are not real.

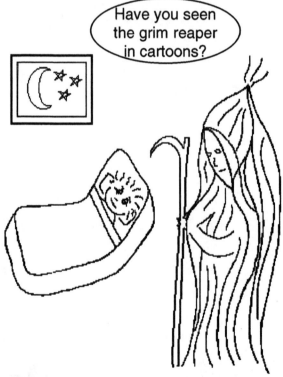

Death can feel like a very scary thing when you don't know what is going to happen. I want to share with you what you **might see**, so death won't be so scary.

As people get closer to death, **their skin color may change.** You will notice they look a slightly different color than they normally do.

There are so many different colors.

Some people look pale, gray, yellow, light brown, ashen, or just lighter than usual. It all depends on what sickness they have and the natural color of one's skin. The skin color will vary from person to person. You will be able to tell the difference.

**Their breathing may change as they get closer to death.** They may breathe faster than normal for a little while. Then their breathing may start to slow down.

They may have a **fever** and get **really hot**, causing them to **sweat a lot**. A cool wet washcloth on the forehead is helpful at this time.

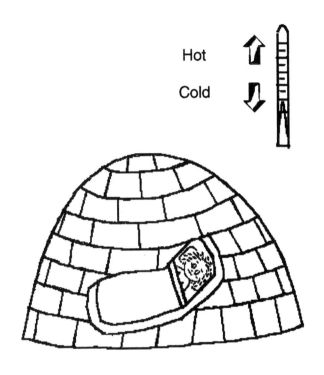

**Near the time of death, their body may start to feel cold to the touch.**

### At the moment and time of death,

they will stop breathing, their heart will stop beating, and all the muscles in their body will relax.

### Death Checklist:

☑ 1 Breathing stops

☑ 2. Heart stops

☑ 3. Muscles relax

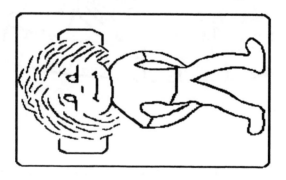

After death, the physical body will lay very still. It will not move anymore. The body will become cold and stiff.

## Food and Drink

They will not need to eat or drink anymore, because dead people don't get hungry or thirsty.

### Food and Drink Checklist:

  1. No more eating

  2. No more drinking

Dead people may look as if they are

sleeping, but we all know that

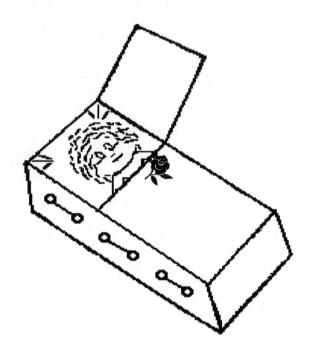

**sleeping is**

**different than death.**

We sleep to feel rested. When we are tired, we take a nap.

When we wake up, we feel rested, have more energy to play, work, and do all the things we want to do.

Sleeping is different than death.

**Dead people**

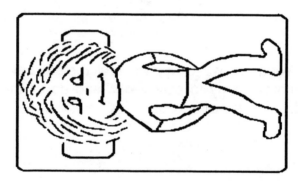

**never wake up.**

Draw or write about what you think might happen after the person you love has died.

**Draw a picture of your family.**

There is
a part of us
that lives on
forever,
even after we die.

Do you know what that part of
us is called?

**The part of us that lives forever is called the soul or spirit.** At the time of death, this soul or spirit leaves the body and is free to go on to have other experiences.

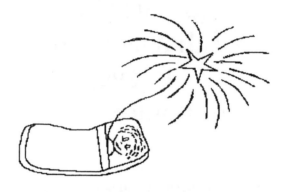

**The soul or spirit is that divine part of us that never dies.** It remembers all the experiences of the past and all love it has ever known.

Draw or write about the soul or spirit.

If you have something to say to someone who has died, **it is never too late.**

In fact, you could take a little time right now to speak to their soul or spirit, and share anything you want. They may not be able to answer you the way they did before, but they will hear you. You might feel better, too.

Draw or write about something you wish you had said to the person you loved. It's OK. Can you think of anything?

That is all I can think of to share with you for now.

## Do you have any other questions that need answers?

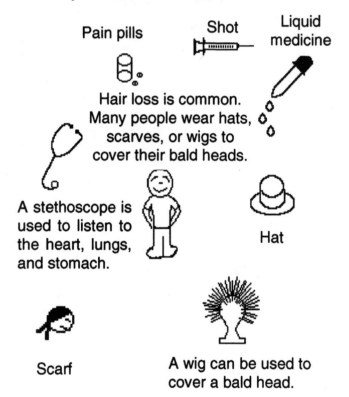

Pain pills

Shot

Liquid medicine

Hair loss is common. Many people wear hats, scarves, or wigs to cover their bald heads.

A stethoscope is used to listen to the heart, lungs, and stomach.

Hat

Scarf

A wig can be used to cover a bald head.

**If you still have questions, be sure to ask someone who knows. It really helps!**

Draw or write about any questions you have that need answers.

It really hurts a lot to lose someone you love. I cried a lot of tears. Sometimes I wish I could see them again. One thing I do know for sure, they will live in my heart forever!

By the way, I'm not afraid of death anymore because I know what to expect, and I have seen people die. It is very peaceful.

**They say it's almost always peaceful.**

Draw or write about a happy time you had with your loved one. Can you think of one?

## Transitions Along the Way
A Guide to the Dying Process
for Children and Young Adults
by
Stephanie A. Jonah, R.N.

---
**Price per book $7.95**
100 or more books @ $6.95 each

**Shipping**
$1.50 for the first book and
.75 cents for each additional book.

---

I would like to order the following:  **Quantity   Amount**

**Transitions Along the Way** _____  $_____

*Please add sales tax       Sales tax _____  $_____
for books shipped to
California addresses.       Shipping _____  $_____

                            **Total** _____

Name_____
Organization _____
Street Address_____
City_____State_____Zip_____
Phone_____

### To place an order
Please mail check or money order to:
Down Time                   Phone: 707-746-8890
P.O. Box 1514               Fax: 707-746-8892
Benicia, California 94510
              ☐ Visa        ☐ Mastercard
Card number: _____
Name on card: _____
Exp. date: _____/_____

-50-